Leonardo da Vinci
1452-1519

Leonardo da Vinci (1452-1519) was born in Italy, the son of a gentleman of Florence. He made significant contributions to many different disciplines, including anatomy, botany, geology, astronomy, architecture, paleontology, and cartography.

He is one of the greatest and most influential painters of all time, creating masterpieces such as the *Mona Lisa* and *The Last Supper*. And his imagination led him to create designs for things such as an armored car, scuba gear, a parachute, a revolving bridge, and flying machines. Many of these ideas were so far ahead of their time that they weren't built until centuries later.

He is the original "Renaissance Man" whose genius extended to all five areas of today's STEAM curriculum: Science, Technology, Engineering, the Arts, and Mathematics.

You can find more information on Leonardo da Vinci in *Who Was Leonardo da Vinci?* by Roberta Edwards (Grosset & Dunlap, 2005), *Magic Tree House Fact Tracker: Leonardo da Vinci* by Mary Pope Osborne and Natalie Pope Bryce (Random House, 2009), and *Leonardo da Vinci for Kids: His Life and Ideas* by Janis Herbert (Chicago Review Press, 1998).

Fascinating World of SCIENCE

Illustrated by
GREG PAPROCKI

Written by
BOB COOPER

GIBBS SMITH
TO ENRICH AND INSPIRE HUMANKIND

SCIENCE is *everything* we know about *everything* in the world . . . and beyond!

SCIENTISTS are curious about *new* things that nobody else knows yet.

You can see lots of things scientists are interested in by simply looking out the window of your house.

Some things are *so far away* we need
TELESCOPES to see them . . .

. . . and others are *so small* we need
MICROSCOPES to see them.

BIOLOGY is the study of all living things, including human beings.

There are **BOTANISTS** that study **PLANTS**, and **ZOOLOGISTS** that study **ANIMALS**.

There are even scientists that study everything they can about just a single thing, like BIRDS, or TREES, or INSECTS, or FISH.

Scientists know more about HUMAN BEINGS
than they do about any other animal.

PHYSIOLOGISTS study all the parts of the human body.

PSYCHOLOGISTS study how we think and behave.

Scientists use machines to look at things inside our bodies that we wouldn't be able to see otherwise, like our BONES, MUSCLES, and ORGANS.

Powerful MICROSCOPES help us see
the tiny MOLECULES and CELLS that bones,
muscles, and organs are made of.

The microscopic cells in our bodies—and everything else in the universe—are made up of millions of even tinier particles called ATOMS.

And atoms are made up of still *tinier* particles, with funny names like UP QUARKS and CHARM QUARKS, which NUCLEAR PHYSICISTS have only recently discovered.

SOCIOLOGISTS and ANTHROPOLOGISTS
study how *groups* of people behave
when they're together.

People who live in different places around the world may do things much differently than you and your family do—like getting married.

Some scientists try to understand what happened in the past from clues that become buried deep in the ground over time.

ARCHAEOLOGISTS dig up remains of old buildings and cities that are sometimes thousands of years old.

PALEONTOLOGISTS dig up bones of animals, called FOSSILS, like those of huge DINOSAURS that lived *millions* of years ago.

From looking at the bones, they can imagine what real live dinosaurs looked like!

There are also scientists who study our whole planet EARTH.

GEOGRAPHERS study things like
MOUNTAINS, OCEANS, and DESERTS.

GEOLOGISTS study the ROCKS that make up the mountains, deserts, and even entire CONTINENTS of Earth.

Our Earth is only a very
small part of the UNIVERSE.

ASTRONOMERS use telescopes
to see other objects in our SOLAR SYSTEM, including
the SUN, the MOON, and other PLANETS,
like JUPITER and MARS.

We can even see beyond our solar system
to other STARS, and even entire GALAXIES.

Scientists enjoy discovering and learning about things.

What kinds of things
do *you* want
to learn about?

What kind of scientist would *you* like to be?

GLOSSARY

ANIMAL: A living thing that is not a plant and can usually move around freely.

ANTHROPOLOGIST (an-throw-PAUL-uh-jist): A scientist who studies humans and their culture.

ARCHAEOLOGIST (are-key-ALL-uh-jist): A scientist who learns about ancient humans and cultures by studying bones, tools, and other clues that are often buried in the ground.

ASTRONOMER (uh-STRON-uh-murr): A scientist who studies the planets, stars, galaxies, and other objects in our universe.

ATOM (AT-um): The smallest particle of matter that can exist by itself. It combines with other atoms to form molecules.

BIOLOGY (by-ALL-uh-jee): The science that deals with all living things, including plants and animals.

BIRD: A type of animal with wings and feathers. Most birds can fly.

BONE: One of the hard pieces that make up the skeleton of some animals' bodies, including humans.

BOTANIST (BOT-uh-nist): A scientist who studies plants.

CELL: The smallest part that makes up all living things.

CONTINENT (CON-tuh-nent): One of the seven large landmasses of Earth: Europe, Asia, Africa, Australia, North America, South America, and Antarctica.

DINOSAUR (DIE-nuh-sore): A type of large reptile that lived millions of years ago but is now extinct.

EARTH: The third planet from the Sun in our solar system—and where we live!

FISH: An animal that lives in water and breathes through gills. Most fish have scales and fins.

FOSSIL (FAW-sull): A piece of a plant or animal that lived long ago that's been preserved in rock, like dinosaur bones or a leaf from a plant.

GALAXY (GAL-uck-see): A large group of stars and their planets. Our solar system is a very small part of the Milky Way galaxy.

GEOLOGIST (jee-ALL-uh-jist): A scientist who studies the rocks, mountains, deserts, and continents of Earth.

HUMAN BEING: A person—like you, for instance!

INSECT: A small animal with six legs. Some insects also have wings.

JUPITER (JEW-puh-durr): The fifth planet from the Sun, and the largest planet in our solar system.

MARS: The fourth planet from the Sun.

MICROSCOPE (MY-cruh-scope): A device used for looking at very small objects so they can be seen clearly.

MOLECULE (MALL-uck-yule): The smallest piece of something that has all the characteristics of that substance. Molecules are made up of atoms.

MOON: The natural satellite that circles the Earth once every 28 days.

MUSCLE (MUSS-ull): A bundle of tissue in humans and animals that contracts, producing movement in parts of the body.

NUCLEAR PHYSICIST (NEW-klee-urr FIZZ-uh-sist): A scientist who studies the parts of an atom's nucleus and the energy that's created when those parts are split apart or joined together.

ORGAN: A part of a human's or an animal's body that has a special function (like the heart or the lungs).

PALEONTOLOGIST (pay-lee-un-TALL-uh-jist): A scientist who studies the fossils of ancient plants and animals, like dinosaurs.

PHYSIOLOGIST (fizzy-ALL-uh-jist): A scientist who studies the physical processes and activities of living things.

PLANET: An object that circles a star (like the Earth, which circles the Sun).

PLANT: A living thing that has roots and grows in the ground. Plants usually have leaves and flowers.

PSYCHOLOGIST (sigh-CALL-uh-jist): A scientist who studies the human mind and human behavior.

QUARK (kwark): A type of very small particle found in an atom's nucleus. Different types of quarks include UP QUARKS and CHARM QUARKS.

ROCK: The hard, solid material that makes up the Earth's surface.

SCIENCE: The knowledge and study of everything in the universe.

SOCIOLOGIST (so-see-ALL-uh-jist): A scientist who studies human society, social institutions, and social relationships.

SOLAR SYSTEM (SO-lurr SIS-tumm): The Sun and all the planets that circle it, including the Earth.

STAR: An object like the Sun that's made of burning gases and produces light. Many stars have their own systems of planets circling them.

SUN: The star that the Earth and the other planets of the solar system circle. Another name for the Sun is SOL (where the word "solar" comes from).

TELESCOPE (TELL-uh-scope): A long tube-shaped device used to see objects very far away.

TREE: A plant with a thick wooden stem and large branches. Trees can grow very tall.

UNIVERSE (YOU-nuh-verse): All of space and everything in it, including galaxies, stars, and planets.

ZOOLOGIST (zoo-ALL-uh-jist): A scientist who studies animals and animal behavior.

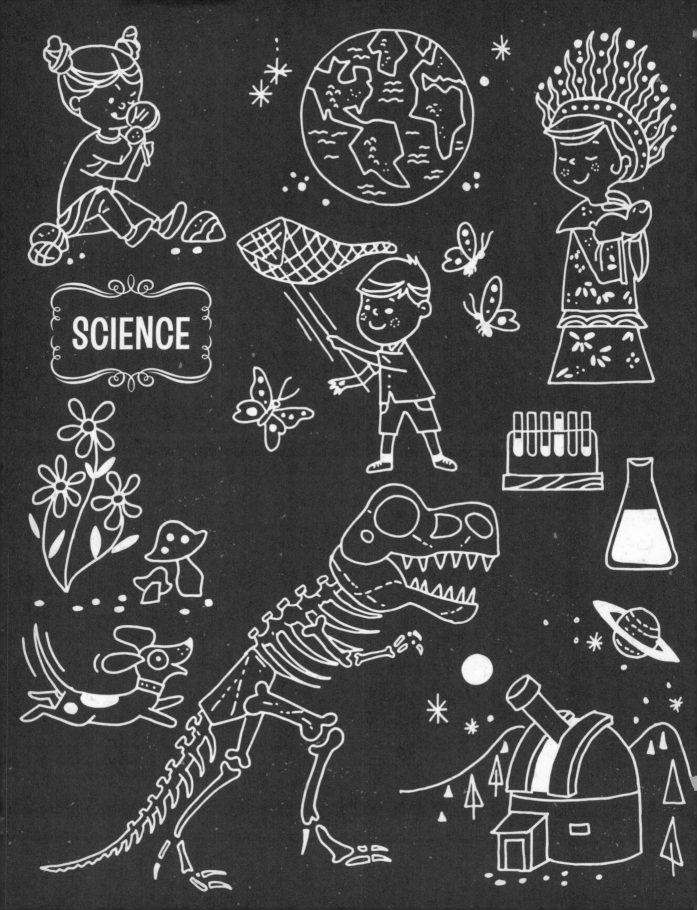

SCIENCE